NOW YOU CAN READ....
DANIEL AND HIS FRIENDS

STORY RETOLD BY LEONARD MATTHEWS

ILLUSTRATED BY HARRY BISHOP

Library of Congress Cataloging in Publication Data

Matthews, Leonard.
  Daniel and his friends.

  (Now you can read—Bible stories)
  Summary: Retells the Bible story of Daniel, whose
faith saved him from fierce lions and his three friends
from a fiery furnace.
  1. Daniel, the Prophet—Juvenile literature.
2.' Prophets—Iraq—Biography—Juvenile literature.
3. Bible stories, English—O.T. Daniel. [1. Daniel,
the Prophet.   2. Bible stories—O.T.] I. Title.
II. Series.
BS580.D2M35   1984   224'.5'0924   [B]   84-15127
ISBN 0-86625-308-4

GROLIER ENTERPRISES CORP.

NOW YOU CAN READ....
DANIEL AND HIS FRIENDS

Six hundred years before Jesus was born, there lived a king named Nebuchadnezzar. He was always looking for new lands to conquer. He took an army to Judah. This country had once been part of Israel. He defeated the armies of Judah. The king ordered many of the people of Judah to leave their homes and live in other lands.

The people of Judah wandered away and settled in many countries. Some settled in Nebuchadnezzar's own country of Babylonia. Among them was a young prince named Daniel.

Daniel was very smart. He was invited to stay in the king's palace.

He was taught by the royal teachers. The king liked him very much.

One night the king had a strange dream. The next morning as he sat up in bed yawning, he tried to remember his dream. He could not, so he sent for his wise men.

"Tell me the meaning of my dream," he told them.

"First tell us your dream, Your Majesty," said one of the wise men.

"I have forgotten it," said the king. "You are supposed to be magicians. If you are, then tell me what I dreamed."

Of course, the wise men could not do this. The king was so angry he ordered all his wise men to be put to death. One of them was Daniel. Daniel was very surprised. He had done nothing wrong. He asked to speak to his friend the king.

Daniel told the king that, the next day, he would tell him his dream and what it meant. The king was pleased. That night Daniel prayed to God. He asked God to help him.

During the night God came and told Daniel all about the king's dream.

Next morning Daniel said to the king, "You dreamed about a great statue. Its head was made of gold. Its arms, legs and feet were made of silver, brass, iron and clay. A great stone came down. It smashed the statue to pieces. Then, the stone began to grow. It grew so big, it became a mountain."

"Daniel, you are right," said the king. "What does it mean?"

"The head of gold is you," replied Daniel. "The other parts are the kings who will come after you."

"And what about the mountain?" the king asked.

"The mountain is the kingdom of God," Daniel told the king, "the kingdom that is to come. Like a mountain, it will never be destroyed. Not even earthquakes will be able to destroy it. It will be there forever."

King Nebuchadnezzar stood in wonder before Daniel. Then he bowed to Daniel.

"I bow to you, Daniel," the king said. "Your God is a great God. He tells you secrets not known to other men. You will be my chief governor."
The king decided not to kill the other wise men because Daniel had told him all about his dream.

Years passed and Nebuchadnezzar died. Soon after, the country was taken over by Darius, King of Persia. He liked Daniel. He made Daniel one of his three leaders.

Many of the princes of Persia did not like Daniel. They were jealous of his friendship with the king. They wanted to get rid of Daniel.

The jealous princes asked the king to make a law. For thirty days no man was allowed to worship any god. It was a foolish law. It was really a trap for Daniel. They knew that Daniel would always pray to his God. The law was passed. The wicked princes watched Daniel until they saw him praying.

Then the princes ran to the king.

"Daniel has broken the law," they told the king. "We have seen him with our own eyes."

The king was upset. He had expected Daniel to obey his law. He did not know what to do.

Daniel was the king's friend and a leader of his country. Finally, the king sent for Daniel. Daniel confessed that he had prayed to his God every day.

Now the king was sure he could not save Daniel.

"You broke one of my laws," the king said sadly. "I cannot change the law."

He called to one of his soldiers.

"Take this man and put him into the den of lions," the king said.

Daniel stared sadly at the king who was his friend.

That night the king could not sleep.
Daniel was taken and put into a den
where there were lions.

"That is the last we will ever see
of Daniel," laughed his enemies.
They were wrong.

While they laughed, Daniel stood
quietly facing the lions.

The lions did not touch Daniel. The next morning, Darius hurried to the den of lions. A surprise was waiting for him there. Daniel was still alive! The king was overjoyed. He gave orders for Daniel to be set free at once.

"Your God has saved you," he said. Daniel smiled and nodded.

"In the future," said the king, "all my people will worship the God of Daniel. His God is all-powerful and the true God." Daniel remained the friend of King Darius until the king died three years later.

In his lifetime Daniel made many good friends apart from Nebuchadnezzar and Darius. He was loved by everyone, for he was a kind ruler until he died.

All these appear in the pages of the story. Can you find them?

Daniel

royal teacher

Nebuchadnezzar

jealous
prince

lion

Darius

Now tell the story in your own words.